# Dollhouse Magic

# DOLLHOUSE MAGIC

*How to Make and Find Simple Dollhouse Furniture*

by P.K. Roche · photographs by John Knott

drawings by Richard Cuffari

The Dial Press · New York

*For my parents and*
*for Jack and Keith — and especially*
*for Janet, with thanks for her help and good ideas*

Text copyright © 1977 by Patricia K. Roche
Pictures copyright © 1977 by Richard Cuffari
Photographs copyright © 1977 by John Knott
All rights reserved | First Printing
Printed in the United States of America
Designed by Jane Byers Bierhorst

Library of Congress Cataloging in Publication Data

Roche, Patricia K
Dollhouse magic.

1. Doll furniture. I. Cuffari, Richard, 1925-
II. Knott, John. III. Title.
TT175.5.R6          745.59′23          76-42932
ISBN 0-8037-2122-6 | ISBN 0-8037-2123-4 lib. bdg.

# CONTENTS

# DOLLHOUSE MAGIC

# Before You Start

A sponge becomes a sofa and a broken watch a clock. A pretty stamp becomes a picture for the wall and a playing card a rug for the floor. All this is a kind of magic, magic that you do yourself — dollhouse magic.

It's easy to make or find wonderful, one-of-a-kind pieces of dollhouse furniture. You begin by thinking small — dollhouse size. Then look around your house for odd bits and pieces. Try imagining different ways to use these odds and ends. A bottle cap can be a pie pan or a picture frame. A toothpaste cap can be a lampshade or a flower pot. A marble is a dollhouse ball or a base for a lamp. A shampoo cap is a stool for a doll.

Ask your family to save small things for you. Keep them in a special box. Every house has different odds and ends, so trade with friends too. You need only a few things to make each piece for your dollhouse. In fact, you don't even need a dollhouse. The last chapter of this book has lots of ideas about what you can use instead.

First read Things to Save and Basic Tools and Materials. And then you'll be ready to start making some very special things.

# Things to Save

beads, all sizes

blocks, small ones

boxes, cardboard or plastic

buttons

candles, birthday size

caps from tubes, jars, and
  bottles

cardboard

charms from key rings or
  bracelets

containers for jelly or milk (from
  restaurants)

decorations from cakes or
  cupcakes

fabric pieces

favors from parties, trinket
  machines, or Cracker Jacks

game pieces

jewelry and parts of it

label stickers

lipstick covers

lollipop sticks

marbles

mirrors — small ones

nutshells

pictures from magazines and
  greeting cards

pipe cleaners

playing cards

postage stamps

ribbons

seashells

souvenirs

spools of thread, empty

thimbles

toys, small ones or pieces from
  old ones

trimmings of braid, lace, and
  eyelet

*Remember…Think Small!*

# Basic tools and materials

*Tools* / scissors

     white glue (Elmer's is fine)

     scotch or double-face tape or both

     ruler

     pencils

     poster paints and brushes

     fine-tipped markers

*Materials* / You may want to buy some of the things that are used in many pieces of furniture: kitchen sponges, matchboxes, map tacks, wire nails (3/4-inch size), extra beads, and clay (colored clay is especially nice to use).

*Before you begin to work:*

1 / Pick out what you want to make.

2 / Read how to do it.

3 / Have all the things you will need to make the piece of furniture set out.

4 / Use old newspaper to work on.

*One very important thing* / Don't be afraid to add to or change things that you've made — or to make something different. It's fun to try out your own ideas!

# A Room to Sit in

**H**ere is one room where the whole doll family will gather. Their friends will come here too. You'll want to make a comfortable sofa for them and perhaps some chairs and a small table or two. If you add a cozy fireplace, this room may become the family's favorite room in the house.

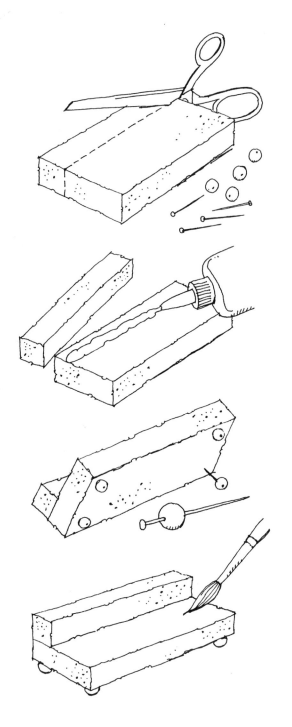

# Plain sofa

*You will need* / a medium-size kitchen sponge

a ruler

a pencil or ballpoint pen

scissors

glue

four 3/4-inch wire nails

four beads

paint, if you like

1 / Measure with the ruler and use the pencil or pen to mark off about one inch on the long side of the sponge.

2 / Wet the sponge and then squeeze it as dry as you can.

3 / Cut the sponge. The long narrow piece that you cut off will be the back of the sofa. Let the sponge dry.

4 / When it is dry, glue the back and seat pieces together.

5 / To make the sofa legs, put a nail through the hole in each bead. Then push a bead and nail into each corner of the sofa.

6 / Paint the sofa if you wish.

# Two easy chairs

*You will need /* a medium-size kitchen sponge

a ruler

a pencil or ballpoint pen

scissors

glue

eight 3/4-inch wire nails

eight beads

paint, if you like

1 / Measure with the ruler and use the pencil to mark a line across the middle of the sponge. Now mark off a narrow piece on each half.

2 / Wet the sponge and squeeze it as dry as you can.

3 / Cut the sponge in half. Next, cut off the narrow piece on each half. These narrow pieces will be the chair backs.

4 / Be sure that the sponge is dry, then use glue to join the back and seat pieces.

5 / For chair legs, put a nail through the hole in each bead. Then push a nail and bead into the corners of each chair.

6 / **Paint the chairs if you like.**

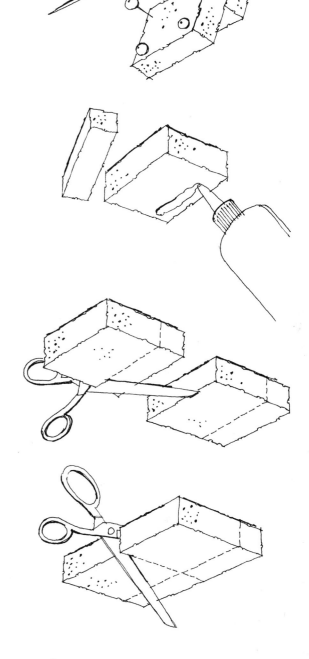

# Covered sofa

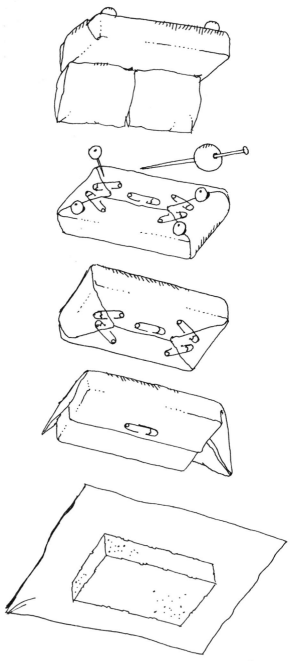

*You will need* / a small kitchen sponge
a piece of soft, lightweight fabric
five small safety pins
four 3/4-inch wire nails
four beads

1 / Think of the sponge as a present that you are wrapping. Lay the sponge flat on the wrong side of the fabric.

2 / Pin the edges of the fabric together at the center of the sponge.

3 / Fold the fabric at one end so that it makes a triangle.

4 / Bring the triangle as close as you can to the first pin that you put in. Pin the triangle to the fabric. Use one or two pins.

5 / Fold and pin the other end.

6 / If you want legs for this sofa, put a nail through the hole in each bead, then push the nail with the bead on it into each corner of the sofa.

7 / Turn the sponge over and add pillows (see page 18).

## More sofa ideas

Do you have a small rectangular gift box? Try it as a covered sofa. Add some pillows. Or you can make a sofa just out of pillows. Make a large pillow for the seat and a few small ones for the back.

# Fireplace and accessories

*The fireplace (ask an adult to help)*

*You will need /* a small gift box

a ruler

a pencil

an X-acto or other sharp knife

glue

paint or markers or pebbles for a stone fireplace

1 / Measure with the ruler and use the pencil to mark an opening on the outside of the bottom section of the box. Make the opening big enough for logs.

2 / Ask an adult to cut out this opening. Cut only on the top of the box. Don't cut through the side of the box.

3 / Put glue on the side of the box below the opening.

4 / Press the cut box onto the box top. Place the cut portion as far back on the box top as possible, so that the front portion of the box top becomes a hearth. Or, instead of the box top, you can use a flat piece of cardboard for the hearth.

5 / Paint the fireplace if you like. Or draw bricks with markers. Or make a stone fireplace.

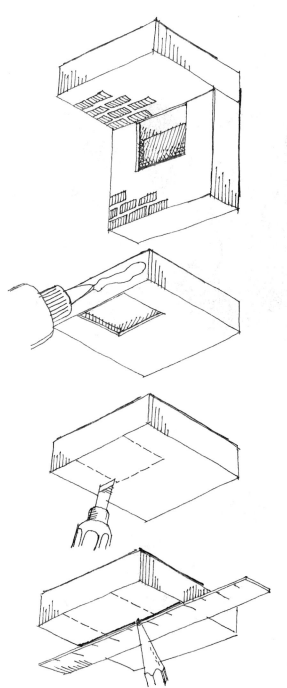

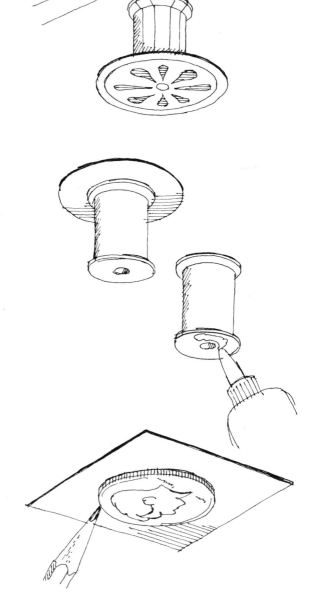

# End table

*You will need /* a fifty-cent piece
cardboard
a pencil
scissors
a small spool
glue
paint or markers

1 / Put the fifty-cent piece on the cardboard and draw around it.
2 / Cut out the cardboard circle.
3 / Put glue on top of the spool.
4 / Press the spool down onto the cardboard circle.
5 / Paint the table, or decorate it with markers.

## More table ideas

In place of the spool, you can use a napkin ring, a block, a cork, a large bead, or a small box to make a table base.

For a different table top, you can try a large flat button, a small mirror or a small box cover. Some of these tops will make coffee tables, which are a little longer and larger than an end table. The bench seat, on page 33, can also be a coffee table.

## A stone fireplace

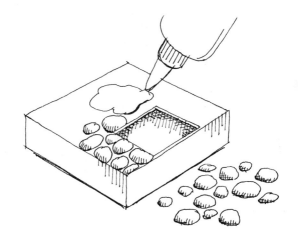

To make a stone fireplace, begin with the front of an already-made fireplace. Apply a great deal of glue in a small area. Then put on several pebbles. The glue that shows looks like mortar between the stones. Let each side dry before doing the next side.

## Things for the fireplace

Twigs are very real-looking logs. Shampoo caps or nut baskets are just right to hold the logs. Game pieces become andirons. Put a vase of flowers, a candle, or a sculpture on the mantel. Hang some pictures or a mirror above it.

# Small Things for Every Room

This chapter tells about all the small things that will make your doll family's rooms especially their own. Add some of these small things to the room to sit in, and you'll see how they change it. Try hanging a picture over the fireplace, put a plant on the mantel, some pillows on the sofa, and a lamp on a table. Put more small things in the other rooms. Your doll family will begin to look very much at home.

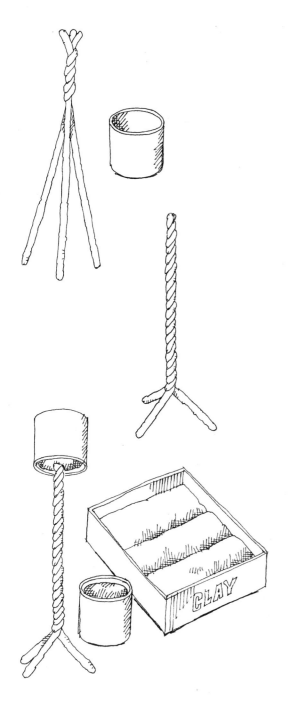

# Lamps

You'll need clay to make each of these lamps. Clay, like glue, holds things together. But if you want to change anything, it's easy to do it with clay.

## *Floor lamp*

*You will need* / three pipe cleaners

a cap from a small bottle

clay

1 / Twist the pipe cleaners together to make a pole, but stop about an inch from the bottom.

2 / Bend out the pipe cleaners three ways so that the lamp pole will stand.

3 / Put some clay into the cap.

4 / Press the top of the lamp pole gently into the cap.

# Table lamp

*You will need* / a cap from a toothpaste tube or other small tube

clay

a marble

1 / Put some clay into the cap.

2 / Gently press the marble into the cap.

3 / Take some more clay, roll it between your palms and flatten it slightly.

4 / Gently press the marble into the clay base.

# More lamp ideas

In place of the marble, you can use a bead, an odd piece from an old game, a bit of old jewelry, a piece of fancy macaroni, a golf tee, a Tinker Toy or Lego piece, a twig, or any small stick.

Instead of a clay base, you can use a small, flat button. Put a little bit of clay in the center of the button to hold the parts together. Press the marble or bead into it.

For a floor lamp, you can use a lollipop stick for the pole. If you do, make a clay shape with a flat bottom. Press the pole into it and add a bottle cap shade. Use a bit of clay to make it stick.

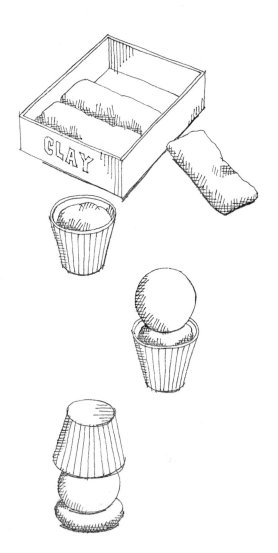

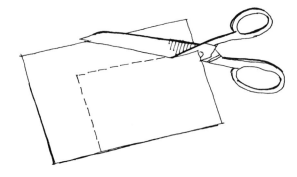

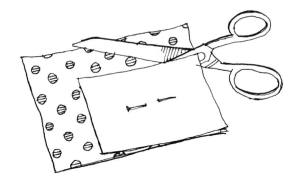

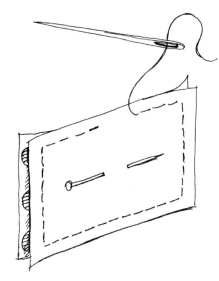

# Pillows

Pompoms, cotton balls, and some powder puffs are good pillows just as they are. But you can make pillows from any soft, lightweight fabric.

*You will need* / a piece of paper
   a ruler
   a pencil
   a piece of fabric
   pins
   a needle and thread
   stuffing (cotton or small strips of fabric)

1 / On the paper draw and cut out a rectangle or square, whichever shape you want your pillow to be. This will be your pattern. Make it larger than you want your finished pillow to be. A pillow looks smaller after it is sewn and stuffed.

2 / Pin your pattern to the fabric and cut around it. Cut a second piece the same way. These will be the pillow's front and back.

3 / Pin the pillow front and back together with the right sides of the fabric on the inside. Sew the pieces together around the edges, but leave a good-size opening for the stuffing.

4 / Pull the unstuffed pillow right side out through the unsewn part.

5 / Gently poke out the corners with a pencil point.

6 / Put stuffing in, a few pieces at a time. Poke it into the corners with a pencil point.

7 / When the pillow is stuffed, fold in the edges of the unsewn part and sew them together.

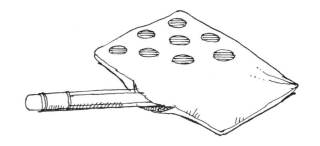

# Pictures, posters, and frames

Pictures for your dollhouse walls can be small drawings that you do yourself or small pictures cut out from magazines or greeting cards. You can even use tiny photos of yourself, your family or friends, or your pet. Stamps make beautiful pictures too.

For posters you can use larger drawings, magazine pictures, stamps, or the backs of small playing cards.

Frames can be lids, bottle caps, toy tires, buttons, checkers, parts of doilies, or heavy, colored paper cut a little larger than the pictures. You can also use a self-stick address label that has a colored edge. Draw your own picture inside.

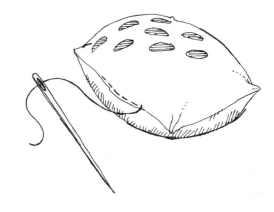

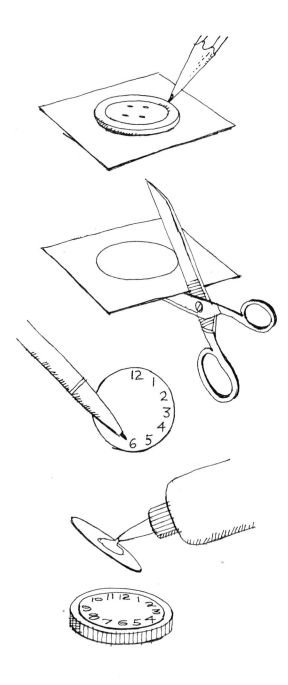

# Clock

A toy watch is a ready-made dollhouse clock, but it's easy to make a clock too.

*You will need* / a flat button or checker
                a smaller button
                heavy paper
                a pencil
                a fine-tipped marker
                glue

1 / Outline the smaller button on the heavy paper and cut out the circle. This will be the face of your clock.

2 / With a fine-tipped marker, draw the numbers and the hour and minute hands on the clock face.

3 / Put glue on the back of the clock face and press it onto the button or checker.

# Mirrors and frames

Use any small mirror, the kind that comes with makeup sets, in compacts, or sometimes in new pocketbooks. If you don't have a mirror, make one. Wrap a piece of aluminum foil around a piece of cardboard. Square or rectangular mirrors are easier to make than round ones.

To make a frame, put a thin line of glue around the mirror edge. Then sprinkle glitter or put candy decorations, seashells, or tiny beads on the glue. Let the glue dry completely before hanging the mirror.

Another kind of frame can be a link from an old belt or curtain or a tire from a toy car. Put glue on the link or tire. Press it onto the mirror. This kind of frame doesn't have to be the same size as the mirror.

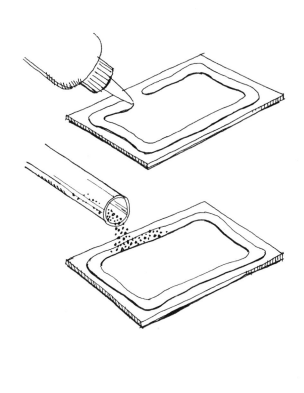

## *How to hang a picture (or clock or mirror)*

You can hang a picture or clock or mirror with a piece of double-face tape. Or roll a piece of scotch tape or masking tape around your pinky, with the sticky side out. Slide it off and press it onto the back of the clock or picture. Press the picture or clock onto the dollhouse wall.

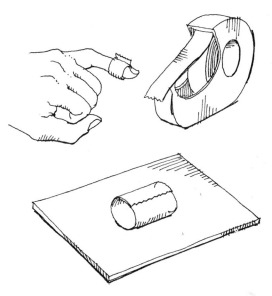

# Flowers, plants, and vases

Flowers and plants in a dollhouse make everything in the dollhouse look more real.

You can use tiny dried straw flowers and put them in vases of toothpaste tube caps, marker tops, thimbles, or lipstick covers. To make the flowers stand as you want them to, put a little clay into the bottom of the vase. Then stick the flowers in, one by one.

You can try a plant cutting in a small container of water or a live plant in a tiny pot — maybe a cactus. But when you are finished playing, take the cuttings and plants out of the dollhouse so they can have sunlight, fresh air, and water.

# Sculpture

You can make your own dollhouse sculpture out of clay. Look at pieces of old toys and jewelry and small game pieces. And don't forget small shells and pebbles. These may be dollhouse sculpture too. If some pieces don't stand by themselves, use a small piece of clay for a base.

# Wastebaskets

A thimble or cap makes the basket. A tiny bit of tissue torn up makes the trash.

# Books and magazines

You can make books and magazines in exactly the same way. Books are a little smaller and a little thicker than magazines.

*You will need* / a piece of lightweight paper

       scissors

       a stapler

       fine-tipped markers or a small picture or stamp and

         glue

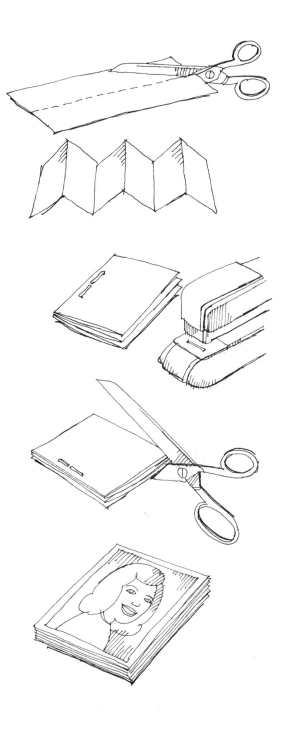

1 / Cut a strip of paper about one to two inches wide and as long as you like — ten inches is a good length. A longer strip will make a thicker book, and a narrower strip makes a smaller one.

2 / Fold the strip of paper like an accordion.

3 / Press the folded strip of paper together and put a staple in one side.

4 / Cut the other side to make even pages.

5 / Draw a picture on the cover with fine-tipped markers. Or glue on a small magazine picture or a stamp.

# Bigger Things for Every Room

**P**ut a rug on your dolls' floor, and you will soon find some of the family or their friends sitting on it. A rug is much nicer than plain floor for playing games, reading a book, or just relaxing.

Windows in dolls' rooms look prettier with a little decoration or curtains hanging in them. If you have one small handkerchief, you can make two sets of curtains.

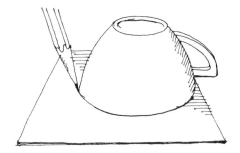

# Rug ideas

## *A yarn circle rug*

*You will need* / a strand of thick yarn (the kind that is sold to tie gifts)

a cup or a small plate

a piece of cardboard

a pencil

glue

a toothpick

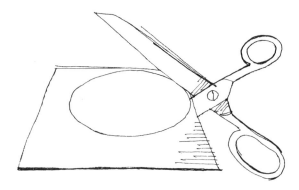

1 / Put the cup or plate upside down on the cardboard and draw around it.

2 / Cut out the circle.

3 / Put glue lightly all over the cardboard circle.

4 / Place one end of the yarn in the center of the cardboard. Gently press the yarn flat. Then wind the yarn around the center and keep winding until you come to the edge of the cardboard. As you wind, hold the yarn flat. Add more glue if you need it.

5 / Take a toothpick and push the end of the yarn under the rug. If the cardboard is too large, trim it with scissors. If the yarn is too long, cut it off.

*You can make rugs from*

1 / scrap pieces of heavy fabric. Fake fur, velvet, tweed, wool, and felt are good kinds to use. If you use felt, you can paint a design on it with poster paints.

2 / a coaster of paper or sisal

3 / a playing card

4 / a paper doily either by itself or glued onto brightly colored paper or fabric

5 / an old washcloth or piece of towel

6 / a scrap of indoor-outdoor carpeting

7 / a postcard that has a pattern on it

8 / a piece from an old place mat, especially the woven kind

9 / paper from a box of candy. (Draw a design on it with markers.)

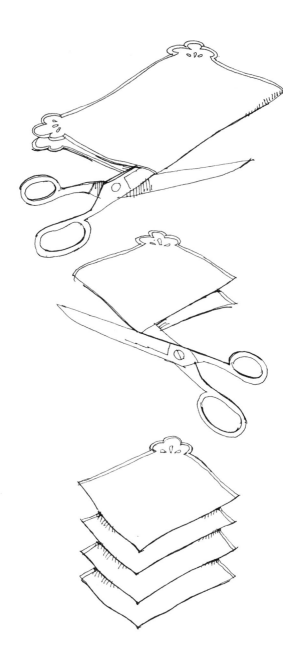

# Curtains and Window Decoration

*Here are some ideas for trimming or covering windows:*

1 / ribbon strips

2 / lace or eyelet edging or braid

3 / corrugated paper (cut it to the right size and paint or decorate it)

## Handkerchief curtains for two windows

This kind of curtain is a good size which will fit many windows.

*You will need* / a small handkerchief

       scissors

       two pipe cleaners

       pins

       a needle and thread

1 / Fold the handkerchief in half. Press the fold down flat with your hand. Then cut the handkerchief along the fold line.

2 / Cut each piece of handkerchief in half again, so that you now have four pieces. Each piece will be half of a pair of curtains.

3 / Take a pipe cleaner and fold one of the curtain pieces over it. Leave enough room to sew a seam and still fit the pipe cleaner rod in after sewing.

4 / Slide out the pipe cleaner, but hold your finger on the folded-over part. Now press the fold down flat with your finger and put in a pin to hold the folded part in place.

5 / Sew a seam near the cut edge of the folded-over curtain piece.

6 / Do steps 3, 4, and 5 for the other three pieces of curtain. When you are finished, hang the curtains on the pipe-cleaner rods. Let the finished or decorated curtain edges be in the middle of the window and the cut edges on the outside.

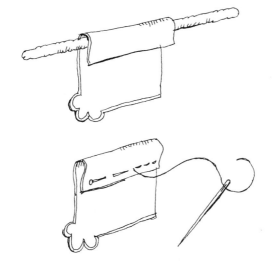

## How to hang curtains or window decorations

Pipe-cleaner curtain rods hang well from small screw eyes. Just push or screw them into the dollhouse wall. (You may need an adult's help.) Then hang the curtains. Screw eyes work with lollipop sticks or round toothpicks too. Besides screw eyes, you can try thumbtacks, pushpins, upholstery nails, or map tacks. Or, depending on what you're hanging, glue or double-face tape may work very well.

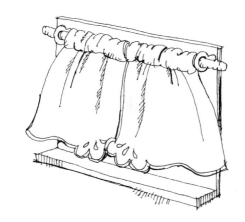

# A Room to Eat in

This is another room that the whole doll family will use. Make a big table for them to eat at and some benches and stools for them to sit on. Or maybe your dolls would like to sit on pillows. Make some candlesticks for the table or a chandelier to hang over it. Then have fun making dollhouse food and deciding how the dolls will serve it.

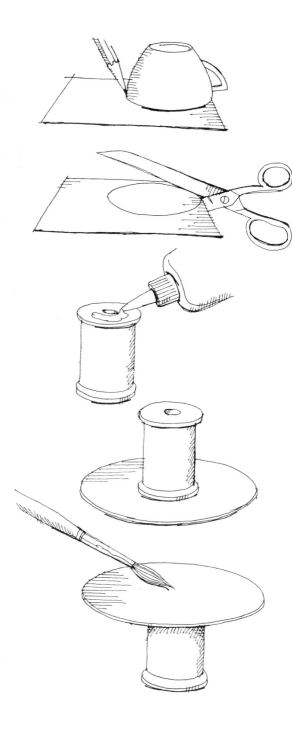

# Round table with tablecloth

## *The table*

*You will need* / a piece of cardboard

a cup

a pencil

a large spool

glue

paint or markers, if you like

1 / Put the cup on the cardboard and draw around it.

2 / Cut out the cardboard circle.

3 / Put glue on top of the spool. Press the spool down onto the cardboard circle.

4 / You can paint this table, decorate it with markers, or make a tablecloth for it.

# The floor-length tablecloth

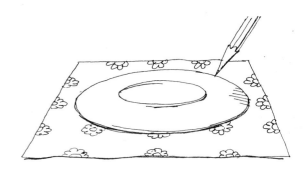

*You will need* / a piece of soft, lightweight fabric

a salad plate (or a saucer if you want a shorter tablecloth)

a pencil

scissors

1 / Put the plate on the cardboard and draw around it.
2 / Cut out the fabric circle.
3 / Put the tablecloth on the table.

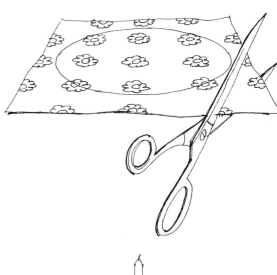

# Seats for dining

Let your dolls sit at their tables on stools, benches or pillows (see page 18). They are easy to find or to make.

For stools, you can use small blocks, large bottle caps (from shampoo bottles), or small cream containers (the kind you get in restaurants). Or try a small lid glued onto a spool.

A small rectangular block makes a good bench. Or you can glue two small spools or blocks to a rectangular seat of cardboard.

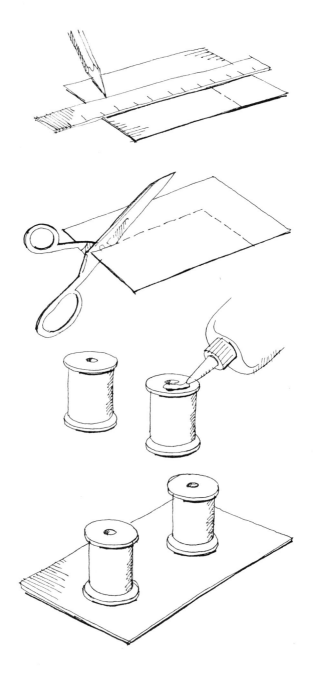

# Large square or rectangular table

This table can be used many ways. A large square table is fine for dining, and so is a rectangular table. A long, narrow rectangular table is good for serving food. It can also be a desk.

*You will need* / a piece of cardboard or a box lid

> a ruler
>
> a pencil
>
> scissors
>
> two large spools or two small blocks
>
> glue
>
> paint or markers
>
> strip of lace or ribbon, if you like

1 / If you have a box lid that is the right size for the tabletop, use it. If not, measure with the ruler and use the pencil to draw the tabletop size on the cardboard.

2 / Cut it out.

3 / Put glue on top of the spools. Press the spools down onto the cardboard.

4 / Paint the table. Or decorate it with markers. Try a strip of lace or ribbon as a runner.

# Candles and candlesticks

*You will need* / a flat button
clay
a birthday candle, used if possible
a knife

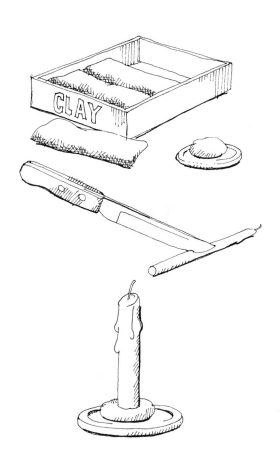

1 / Press a little clay onto the button.
2 / Cut the birthday candle in half. (Used birthday candles look more real.)
3 / Press the candle into the clay.

You can also make a candlestick table. Put a candle into a birthday candle holder. Put the candle and holder into a small spool or large bead.

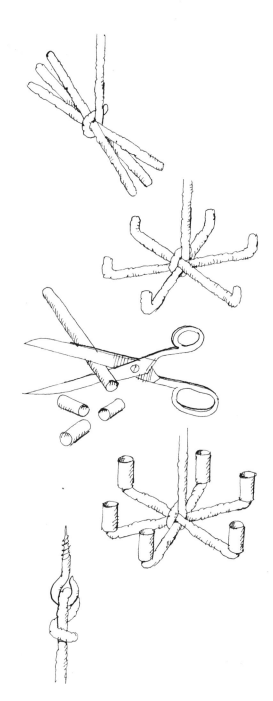

# Chandelier

*You will need* / four pipe cleaners

               scissors

               a drinking straw

               a small screw eye

1 / Hold three of the pipe cleaners together. Wrap the end of the fourth pipe cleaner around the middle of the three pipe cleaners.

2 / Fan out the three pipe cleaners and bend up the tip of each.

3 / To make candles, cut a piece of straw about the size of the bent part. Cut five more pieces of straw the same size as the first piece.

4 / Put a piece of straw on each bent-up pipe-cleaner tip.

5 / Hang the chandelier with a small screw eye. Ask an adult to help. Pull the pipe cleaner through the screw eye until the pipe-cleaner stem is the right length for the room. Twist any extra stem around the main stem.

# Food

Many things make real-looking and sometimes good-tasting doll-house food. Tiny candies and cake decorations make delicious, colorful dollhouse cookies and other desserts. Cheerios are doughnuts on a doll's plate. Dried parsley flakes are salad and small white beans look just like eggs.

If you want a fried egg, use a little white clay with a bit of yellow clay on top. Yellow beads are dollhouse grapefruit and smaller red beads, apples. Try out different size beads, small pebbles, and colored clay for other kinds of food. You can color the pebbles with markers.

# Dishes, bowls, glasses, and trays

Buttons, seashells, and nutshells can be dishes or bowls. Tops from old markers make colorful glasses. Metal and plastic lids (from dry mustard and hot chocolate mix containers) become pretty trays. So do plastic jelly containers. Plastic trinket containers from vending machines are good salad bowls. Bottle caps look like pie tins if you put in some clay pie. Or line the cap with white clay and press tiny red or blue beads into the clay for an open berry pie.

Look at old toys for ideas. The sugar bowl from a small china tea set might be an elegant soup tureen. And don't forget clay. You can use it to make all kinds of dishes, bowls, and trays.

# A Room to Work and Play in

This is the room where the doll family keep their books, toys, and games. Some of them like to do homework here. Start by making a big, comfortable desk. Try a piano with its own stool. This room also needs a sofa for curling up and a big rug for stretching out.

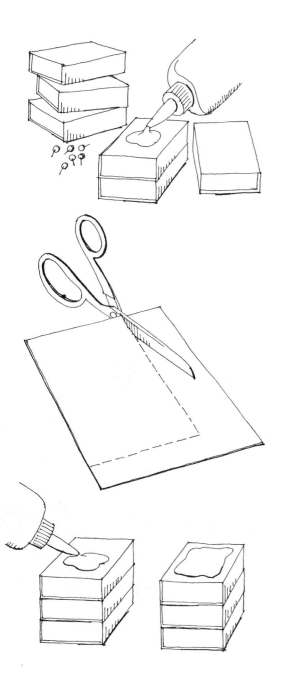

# Desk

*You will need* / six matchboxes

glue

a piece of cardboard

a ruler

a pencil

scissors

paint, if you like

six map tacks

1 / Glue together three of the matchboxes, one on top of the other.

2 / Glue together the other three matchboxes in the same way. Let everything dry.

3 / Draw and cut out a cardboard rectangle big enough to cover the two stacks of boxes and also leave enough space in between them for knees.

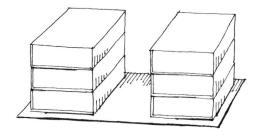

4 / Put some glue on top of each stack of matchboxes. Press the matchboxes down at either end of the cardboard.

5 / If you like, paint the desk.

6 / Press a map tack into the center of each drawer. (A little push on back of a drawer helps it to slide out easily.)

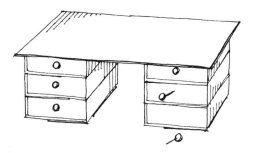

---

Some desk-top things for your dolls to use are a lamp, a phone, a clock, a book, or a few small pieces of paper for writing. You can make two pencils by snapping off the ends of a colored plastic toothpick. A small piece of blotter makes a handsome dollhouse desk blotter.

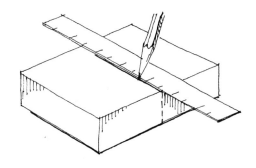

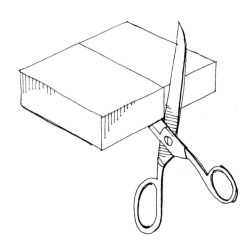

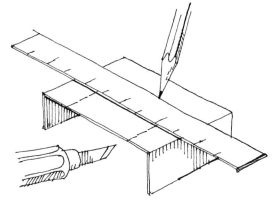

# Piano and Stool

## *The piano (ask an adult to help)*

This upright piano is made from a gift box, both top and bottom. The box bottom is the upright part. You don't need to do anything to the box bottom except attach the keyboard to it.

*You will need /* a small square gift box
a ruler
a pencil
sharp scissors or an X-acto knife
masking tape
paint
a strip of paper
a black marker
glue or double-face tape

1 / To make the keyboard, you will use a little more than one-half of the box top or cover. Measure with the ruler and use the pencil to draw a line slightly above the middle of the box cover.
2 / Ask an adult to cut the box. (Save the leftover piece of box for something else.)

3 / Now measure with the ruler and use the pencil to mark a wide rectangular area. One of the long sides of the rectangle should be along the cut side of the box top. When this rectangular piece is cut out, the remaining part will be the piano's legs and the keyboard.

4 / Ask an adult to cut out this rectangular opening.

5 / Use masking tape to attach the keyboard part of the piano to the upright part along the piano sides.

6 / Paint the piano.

7 / While the piano dries, make a keyboard from a strip of paper. Attach it with glue or double-face tape.

## The piano stool

Glue a leather button onto a small spool for your doll's piano stool. If you want a bench, try a small rectangular block. You can also glue two small spools to a rectangular seat of cardboard.

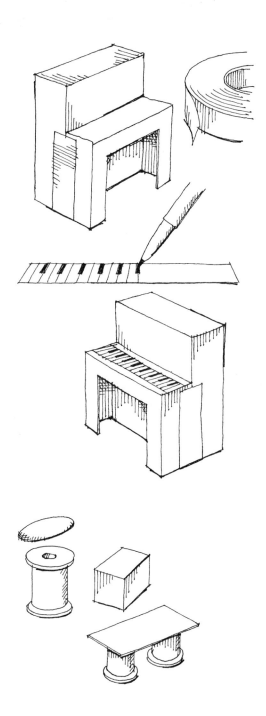

# Toys and games

Dollhouse toys and games come from

1 / pieces of your old toys or small toys themselves
2 / small game pieces
3 / Cracker Jack favors
4 / trinket machines (save the containers too — they make good
    bowls and lampshades)
5 / birthday party favors
6 / decorations or parts of them (cake or holiday decorations)
7 / pieces of old jewelry

If you have a marble, it will be a ball for your dollhouse. Think small and look around your room. See what else you can find.

    Dolls' games and puzzles are easy and fun to make. You can draw a board for chess or checkers on a label or small piece of heavy paper. Use tiny beads or cupcake decorations for chess pieces or checkers. For a dollhouse jigsaw puzzle, try drawing or pasting a picture on a piece of heavy paper or an index card. Then cut it into puzzle pieces.

# Toy chests

See-through plastic boxes make good toy chests. In fact, almost any small box and cover will make a fine toy chest. You can paint cardboard or decorate it with markers.

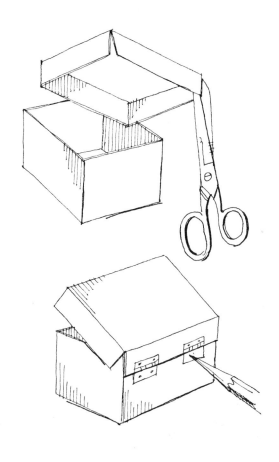

# A hinged toy chest

You might also like to make a hinged toy chest.

*You will need* / a small box

               scissors

               paint or markers, if you like

               scotch tape

1 / Cut two corners of the box lid.

2 / If you are going to paint or decorate the box with markers, do it now. Then draw on hinges. You can draw on a lock as well.

3 / Tape the cut side of the lid to the box bottom.

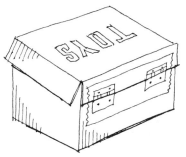

# A Room to Sleep in

Of course the most important thing in this room will be the bed or beds. But what kind would your dolls like? You can make them a pretty covered bed, an old-fashioned four-poster, or a set of bunk beds with a ladder. Make a cradle too, and then perhaps a little bed for the family pet. You can also make your doll family chests of drawers — tall ones or small ones, whatever they need.

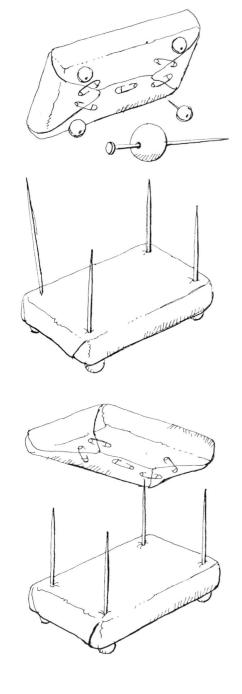

# Covered bed

You make a covered bed the same way that you make a covered sofa (see page 9). The difference is in where you put the pillow — at one end — and in what kind of lightweight fabric you pick to cover the bed. And of course you'll want to make a blanket or spread to put over the bed.

# Bunk beds and ladder

### Bunk beds

*You will need* / two covered beds
four 3/4-inch nails
four beads
four round toothpicks

1 / For the legs of the bottom bunk bed, put a nail through the hole in each bead. Then push a bead and nail into each corner of the bed.
2 / Take this bed and push a toothpick into each corner of its top.

3 / Place the other bed gently on top of the toothpicks. Then hold one of the toothpicks with one hand and press the top bed down onto it with the other hand. Do only one corner at a time.

4 / Add pillows (see page 18).

## The ladder

*You will need* / six pipe cleaners
                   scissors

1 / Twist two pipe cleaners together. Then twist two more together. These are the sides of the ladder.

2 / For the steps, take two pipe cleaners and cut each one in half.

3 / Lay a pipe cleaner step over the two sides of the ladder. Wrap each side of the step around a side of the ladder. Make three more steps, spaced evenly.

4 / At one end of the ladder, bend the pipe-cleaner sides to make hooks.

5 / Hang the ladder from the top bunk. Cut it off to the right length.

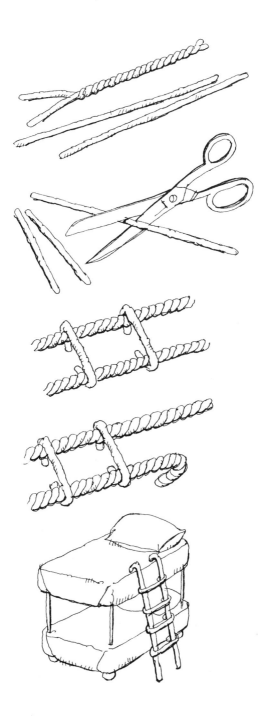

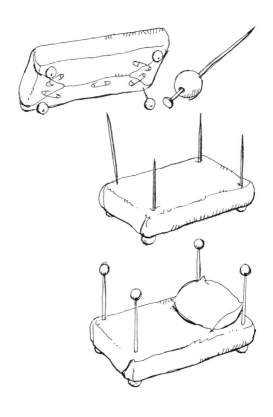

## Four-poster bed

*You will need* / a covered bed

four 3/4-inch wire nails

four plain beads

four round toothpicks

four pretty beads

1 / For the legs of the bed, put a nail through the hole in each bead.
Then push a bead and nail into each corner of the bed.

2 / Push a toothpick into each corner of the bed's top.

3 / Put a pretty bead on top of each toothpick.

4 / Add a pillow (see page 18).

# Bed covers

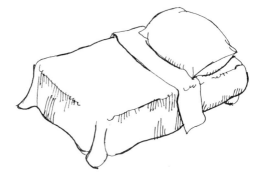

You can make soft, warm bed covers from old doll or baby blankets,
or from your own old night clothes, or from any soft, lightweight
fabric.

# Cradle

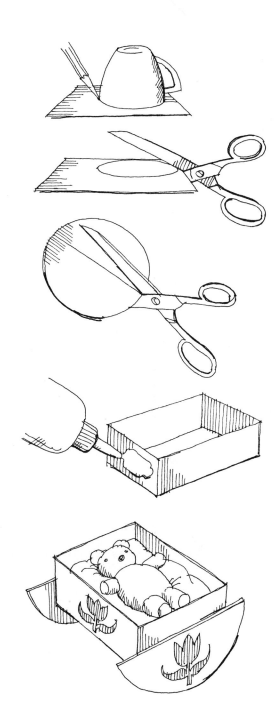

*You will need* / a piece of cardboard

a cup

a pencil

scissors

a small box with no cover

glue

paint or markers

a piece of soft fabric

1 / Put the cup upside down on the cardboard and draw around it.

2 / Cut out the cardboard circle.

3 / Cut the circle in half.

4 / Put glue on each end of the box.

5 / Then press one half circle onto each end of the box.

6 / Paint the cradle or decorate it with markers.

7 / Fold the soft fabric and put it into the cradle.

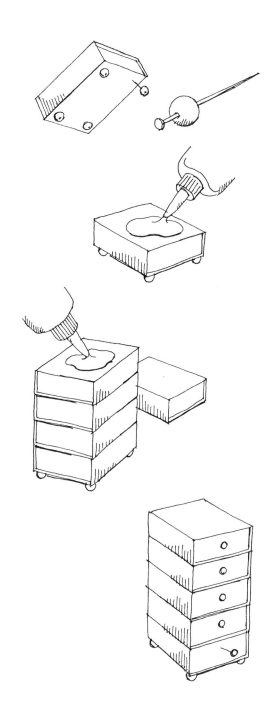

# Chests of drawers

## Tall chest of drawers

*You will need* / four 3/4-inch wire nails

four beads

about five small matchboxes

glue

paint, if you like

five map tacks

1 / If you want legs on your tall chest, put a nail through the hole in each bead. Then push a nail and bead into each corner of a matchbox. (This will be the bottom drawer and will not open.)

2 / Put glue on top of this matchbox and press another matchbox onto it. Glue and press on the other matchboxes. Let them dry.

3 / If you like, paint the chest of drawers.

4 / Press a map tack into the center of each drawer to make a drawer knob.

## Ideas for small chests of drawers

If you make two sets of two glued matchboxes, you'll have a pair of matching night tables. If you glue those two matchbox stacks together side by side you'll have a double dresser. Cut out a dresser top from cardboard and glue it on. Hang a mirror over the dresser.

# Pet bed

*You will need* / a small box or box cover

paint or markers

a piece of soft fabric

1 / Paint or decorate the box with markers.

2 / Fold the soft fabric and put it into the pet bed.

# A blanket chest

If you would like a blanket chest for extra bed covers, make one like the hinged toy chest (see page 45). Try painting it a solid color. Let that dry, then paint a decoration on it in another color.

If you'd like a cushioned window seat, make a pillow (see page 18) for the top of the blanket chest. Draw the pillow pattern a little larger than the top of the blanket chest. Use double-face tape or glue to attach the pillow to the chest.

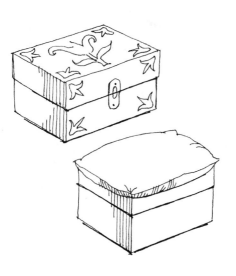

# Dollhouses That Don't Come from Stores

**S**ome of the nicest dollhouses don't come from stores. In fact, some wonderful dollhouses aren't really "houses" at all. Look around your own house. Think about places that would make good dollhouse space.

Here are some ideas for starters. Some of these dollhouses can go with you for visits. Or you can find a place to set up a dollhouse anywhere you go.

1 / A large gift box makes a good one-room dollhouse. Try a shoe box or an ice-skate box for other one-room dollhouses. This kind of dollhouse travels well.

2 / A cardboard grocery box. If the box has a cardboard divider, your dollhouse already has two rooms. If you want more floors, add more boxes. Paint them. Draw in windows and doors and cut them out if you like. One grocery box is easy to carry to a friend's house.

3 / Bookcase shelves. Each shelf becomes a floor of your house. You can divide a shelf by wedging in walls of cardboard. Ask an adult to help. A whole bookcase makes a wonderful dollhouse.

4 / Steps can be dollhouses too — at least for a while. Use part of a stoop or porch steps for a dollhouse outside on a warm, sunny day.

## About the Author

P.K. Roche was born in Brooklyn, New York. She received a B.A. in English from St. John's University. She is interested in illustrating as well as writing children's books and has studied at the New School with Carla Stevens and with Uri Shulevitz.

Ms. Roche has always loved dollhouses. As a child she enjoyed a dollhouse which arrived in move-in condition one Christmas morning. Of just about equal importance, however, was a second dollhouse, a cigar box, which she filled with small furniture of her own making.

Ms. Roche lives in Brooklyn Heights, New York, with her husband and their two children, Janet and Keith.

## About the Photographer

John Knott is a professional photographer; this is his first book for children. He lives in upstate New York.

## About the Artist

Richard Cuffari is the award-winning illustrator of many books for children, including *The Heritage Sampler* (Dial). He lives in Brooklyn, New York.